German Potato Salad | Page 44-45

ONE POT MEALS

Everyday Meals Cooked in Your Mini Rice Cooker

From the Editors at Dash with
Catherine-Gail Reinhard & Jenny Dorsey

StoreBound 50 Broad Street, New York, NY 10004

ISBN 978-0-9971012-2-5

Designed in New York City. Printed in China
10 9 8 7 6 5 4 3 2 1

Distributed by StoreBound
50 Broad Street, New York, NY 10004

Editorial Director Catherine-Gail Reinhard
Executive Food Editor Jenny Dorsey
Editorial Assistants Isabelle Rabin
Art Director Matthew Pisane with Florence Ko
Photography Jenny Dorsey
Staff Photographer Julian Master

Pictured on the Front Cover: Salmon Bibimbap Ingredient Prep by Julian Master
Pictured on the Back Cover: Salmon Bibimbap | Page 22-23

HAPPINESS IS HOMEMADE

Helping you eat better is at the core of everything we do. That's why we make products to help you cook delicious homemade meals. We believe in unprocessed living & that there's no substitute for food cooked with love.

Dash

Quinoa Taco Bowl | Page 56-57

TABLE OF CONTENTS

I'll admit it. When I first used our Mini Rice Cooker I thought it would be a nice little appliance for making healthy side dishes. After many months of testing with our team, and with over 50 recipes developed, I've come to see this compact wonder as a valuable member of my kitchen and worthy of a spot in my countertop (and if you could see my NYC kitchen, you'd know that counter space is at a premium).

And I'm not the only one—from friends and family to our online community, this pint-sized cooker has quickly become a favorite go-to for whipping up everything from chicken curry (page 80-81), to couscous (page 62-65), to quinoa bowls (page 56-57), to banana bread (page 94-95).

We've found that it's not only great for small spaces, but also for portion control. Because let's face it, when was the last time that you made a loaf of banana bread and didn't finish it within a few days? The goal in writing this book is to expand the way that you think about the Mini Rice Cooker and inspire you to get cooking.

From the dorm room to apartment-living, from your RV to boating, the Mini Rice Cooker is a go-anywhere tool that fits into the way we live today. At Dash, we're all about practical solutions to get you into the kitchen and cooking delicious, unprocessed food. So jump in and experiment—we believe there are no mistakes in cooking, only learning experiences (and believe me, I've had plenty of those). Happy cooking!

Catherine-Gail Reinhard
Executive Editor & VP, Product Strategy

How do rice cookers work?

Standard rice cookers have a built-in mechanical thermostat that regulates the temperature based on the boiling temperature of water. Since water boils at 212°F (100°C), as long as there is water in the pot, the temperature cannot go over 212°F. Once all the water or liquid has been absorbed by the rice or grains, the temperature can rise over 212°F and it's at this point that the thermostat switches off. Fancier rice cookers have circuit boards that can run programs that optimize the time and temperature based on the type of rice or porridge being cooked but for all the recipes in this book, a good old-fashioned rice cooker (like our Dash Mini Rice Cooker) will work just fine.

Keep warm - what does that mean?

Once the thermostat has exceeded 212°F, many cookers will switch into "Keep Warm" mode which holds the temperature around 150°F (65°C). Cookers with a Keep Warm function are versatile little cookers that can also be used for light baking tasks.

On this page top to bottom:

Proper Technique

1. WASH: Determine if the type of rice you are using should be rinsed first. Many people believe that rinsing long and medium grain rice will reduce the stickiness and improve the texture of the rice. Rinsing your rice will remove any surface debris on the rice. To rinse your rice, use a strainer and rinse with cool water. One exception is Arborio rice for risotto. For risotto, the extra starch is desirable and adds to the glutenous, creamy texture.

2. MEASURE: Use the correct ratio of liquid to water for the type of rice or grain you are cooking. Too much water can result in gluey rice, too little can result in rice that's too chewy. Observe the goldilocks method (or the tables we've provided) and then adjust to your liking. One important thing to note: the measuring cup that comes with rice cookers is not a standard measuring cup and therefore, if you use that cup, you'll want to use a ratio of liquid to grain instead of standard measures.

3. FLUFF! - After your rice has cooked and your rice cooker switches to "Keep Warm," you should let it rest for a few minutes before fluffing with a fork. Introducing air to the rice not only helps it cool, but also improves the texture. For sushi rice, use a rice paddle to scoop the rice and cool the rice. Sushi chefs often use a fan to bring the temperature of the rice down to the perfect temperature for making sushi.

Baking and Recipes that Require Multiple Cycles

Rice cookers can also be used for light baking tasks. We've included several baking recipes in this cookbook. Generally, light, yeast-free batters work best like those used for pancakes and quickbreads. You may need to run the rice cooker for multiple cycles when baking in order to ensure that your cake is fully baked. As a general rule of thumb, the cake is ready when you insert a toothpick into the center of the cake and it comes out clean.

Setting a Timer for Liquid Recipes

For recipes that are liquid based, the rice cooker will cook continuously till all the liquid is absorbed. For soups, stews, curries and chilis, set a timer so that you keep track of how long you are cooking your food and can switch the cooker to "Keep Warm" manually.

On this page:
Summer Wheat Berry Salad | Page 66-67

3

Grain Cooking Chart

In the following chart we have listed several types of grains along with their ideal water to grain ratio. Measurements are based on a standard measuring cup, not the included Measuring Scoop.

TYPE OF GRAIN	DRY GRAIN	WATER
White Rice	1 cup	1 ¼ cups
Long Grain Brown Rice	1 cup	1 ½ cups
Short Grain Brown Rice	¾ cup	1 ½ cups
Quinoa	¾ cup	1 ½ cups water or broth
Sushi Rice	½ cup	¾ cup
Barley	½ cup	1 ½ cups
Oats (steel cut)	¾ cup	2 cups
Oats (rolled)	¾ cup	1 ¼ cups
Farro	1 cup	2 ½ cups
Wild Rice	1 cup	3 cups

Types of Rice & Other Grains

TYPE OF GRAIN	WHAT IS IT?	CULINARY USES
Arborio Rice	Italian short-grain rice that is large and produces a bold flavor.	Risotto, arancini, minestrone.
Basmati Rice	Long-grain rice grown in India and Pakistan. Fragrant and includes an aging process.	Best served with curries, vegetables, and warm spices.
Jasmine Rice	Originally from Thailand, jasmine rice is floral and slightly sticky when cooked.	Delicious with spicy curries or dried fruit.
Brown Rice	Includes short and long-grain varieties, and is packed with nutrients. Has a rich, nutty flavor.	Can be a substitute for any dish containing white rice, like stir-fry or rice and beans.
Sushi Rice	Brown or white Japanese short-grain rice. Has a high starch content to create the necessary stickiness for sushi.	Sushi! Can also be used in desserts like sweet rice pudding.
White Rice	Basic, long-grain white rice that is fluffy and versatile.	Enjoy it in pilafs, as part of a salad, or top with chicken, meat, or more veggies.
Wild Rice	This grain is actually a grass! Wild rice has a unique texture and a yummy toasty flavor.	Make a fresh wild rice salad with vegetables, or mix with nuts and dried fruit for an addictive side dish.
Black Rice	Flavorful and rich in nutrients, varieties include Indonesian Black Rice and Thai Black Rice.	Try combining forbidden rice with mushrooms and fragrant spices for a hearty main dish.
Farro	A type of wheat, farro is slightly chewy like barley. It is an ancient grain, and rich in nutrients.	Incredibly versatile, farro can be a side dish, tossed with a salad, or even incorporated into a breakfast dish.
Barley	Super healthy and high in fiber and protein, barley is a whole grain with a texture and flavor similar to brown rice.	Enjoy barley soup, or pair with vegetarian curry or vegetable stir-fry for a healthy weeknight dinner.
Quinoa	Quinoa is, in fact, a seed that is prepared like any regular grain. Tasty and highest in protein, quinoa is gluten-free and cholesterol free.	Prepare for quinoa salad, vegetable stir-fry, and even cook for a healthy, hot breakfast!

Quinoa Breakfast Bowl With Hard-boiled Eggs | Page 16-17

BREAKFAST

CHEESY GRITS

Ingredients

- ½ cup quick-cooking grits
- 2 tbsp yellow onion, minced
- 2 cloves garlic, minced
- 1 tsp unsalted butter
- 1 tsp Dijon mustard

- ½ cup cheddar cheese, shredded
- 1 cup whole milk
- ½ cup water
- 2 bay leaves (optional)

Directions

Add all ingredients to the Rice Cooker and stir to combine. Cook for 1 cycle. Once finished, stir the grits with a spoon to incorporate. Remove bay leaves before serving, if needed.

Use a sharp cheddar for a punchier grits, a smooth cheddar for creamy grits.

ZUCCHINI & TOMATO POLENTA

Ingredients

- ½ cup dry polenta
- 10 grape or cherry tomatoes, halved
- 2 tbsp yellow onion, minced
- ⅓ cup zucchini, small dice
- 4 sun-dried tomatoes, chopped
- 1 ½ tsp kosher salt

- 2 dashes ground black pepper
- 1 tsp unsalted butter
- 1 cup low-sodium chicken or vegetable stock
- 1 tbsp basil leaves, sliced

Directions

Add everything except the basil to Rice Cooker and stir to combine. Cook for 1 cycle. Once finished, stir in basil leaves.

You can make sun-dried tomatoes at home - simply slice grape or cherry tomatoes in half and dehydrate overnight!

MUESLI

Ingredients

- ½ cup quick-cooking whole rolled oats
- ¼ cup dried white mulberries
- ¼ cup sliced almonds
- 1 tbsp cacao nibs
- 1 tbsp sunflower kernels
- 1 tbsp goji berries

- 1 tbsp coconut flakes
- 1 tsp wheat germ
- 1 tsp ground flaxseed
- 1 tbsp maple syrup
- ½ cup unsweetened almond milk
- 1 dash ground cinnamon

Directions

Add everything to Rice Cooker and stir to combine. Cook for 1 cycle.

 You can substitute your own favorite berries or nuts for this recipe to make it your own.

BLACK SESAME PORRIDGE

Ingredients

- ¼ cup black sesame seeds
- ¼ cup white jasmine rice
- 1 ½ cups milk or non-dairy milk
- 2 tbsp cane sugar
- mixed berries (optional)

Directions

Combine black sesame seeds and jasmine rice in spice grinder. Grind until consistency resembles that of coarse sand. Transfer to Rice Cooker. Add milk and cane sugar, stir. Cook for 1 cycle. Once finished, serve with mixed berries, if desired.

GIANT FLUFFY PANCAKE

Ingredients

- 1 cup pancake mix
- 1 cup water, milk, or non-dairy milk
- 1 tbsp canola or coconut oil
- maple syrup (optional)
- mixed berries (optional)

Directions

Combine pancake mix, water or milk, and oil in a small bowl. Whisk together thoroughly to incorporate. Pour ½ of mixture into the Rice Cooker. Cook for 2 cycles. Once finished, invert pancake onto plate and serve with maple syrup and berries, if desired. For the second pancake, repeat the process with the other half of the mixture. Makes 2 pancakes.

SUPERFOOD OATMEAL

Ingredients

- ½ cup rolled oats
- 1½ cups water or milk
- 1 tbsp honey or maple syrup
- ½ banana, sliced
- ¼ cup pecans, chopped
- ¼ cup blueberries
- 1 tsp ground flax seeds

Directions

Add oats and water or milk to the Rice Cooker and stir to combine. Cover with Lid and turn the Rice Cooker on. When oats are cooked, add honey or maple syrup and pour into a bowl. Top with ground flax seeds and then banana, chopped pecans, and blueberries.

SUNRISE FRITTATA

Ingredients

- ¼ cup frozen spinach
- 3 tbsp onion, diced
- 3 tbsp tomato, diced

- ¼ cup cheddar cheese, shredded
- 3 large eggs
- salt and pepper, to taste

Directions

Chop the spinach, onion, and tomato. In a bowl, beat the eggs until uniform and then add the cheese.

Press the cook switch on the Rice Cooker and add the vegetables to the cooking bowl. Let cook for 2 minutes with the Lid until the onions are softened. If there is extra water from the vegetables, drain the water before adding the egg.

Pour the egg and cheese mixture over the vegetables and stir once. Cover with the Lid and let cook until the end of the cooking cycle.

QUINOA BREAKFAST BOWL WITH HARD-BOILED EGGS

Ingredients

- ½ cup dry quinoa
- ½ cup radish, chopped
- ½ cup broccoli florets
- ¼ cup sun-dried tomatoes, chopped
- ½ tsp kosher salt
- 1 dash ground black pepper

- 5 oz water or low-sodium chicken or vegetable stock
- 2 large eggs
- 1 cup spinach
- 1 tbsp chives, sliced

Directions

Combine quinoa, radish, broccoli, tomato, salt, pepper and water or stock in the Rice Cooker. Stir to mix thoroughly. Wash eggs and place directly into Rice Cooker. Cook 1 cycle. Remove eggs and carefully peel under running water. Toss cooked quinoa mix with spinach and chives. Serve with peeled eggs.

DUTCH BABY

Ingredients

- ¾ cup whole milk or non-dairy milk
- ½ cup all purpose flour
- 3 large eggs
- ¼ tsp salt
- ¼ tsp vanilla extract
- ¼ cup cane sugar
- powdered sugar (optional)
- 2 lemon wedges (optional)

Directions

Combine all ingredients except powdered sugar and lemon in blender and blend until smooth. Spoon approximately ½ cup into Rice Cooker. Cover and cook 2 cycles. Serve with powdered sugar and lemon wedges, if desired. Makes 4 to 6 servings.

ONE POT MEALS

SALMON BIBIMBAP

Ingredients

- ½ cup short grain white rice
- ½ cup shiitake mushroom, sliced
- ¼ cup carrot, sliced thinly
- ¼ cup mung bean sprouts
- ¼ cup kimchi, sliced thinly
- 1 tsp sesame oil
- 5 oz low-sodium chicken or vegetable broth

- 1 tbsp gochujang or red chili paste
- 2 tsp soy sauce
- 1 4 oz filet skinless salmon
- ½ cup watercress
- ½ tsp white or black sesame seeds
- 1 tbsp toasted nori strips
- 2 tsp scallion, sliced thinly

Directions

Combine rice, mushroom, carrot, mung bean, and kimchi in the Rice Cooker. Mix sesame oil, chicken broth, gochujang (or red chili paste) and soy sauce in a small bowl and whisk to combine. Pour into Rice Cooker. Add salmon to Rice Cooker. Cook 1 cycle. Add watercress and re-cover Rice Cooker to let steam, 1 minute. Add sesame seeds, nori strips, scallion and stir to combine.

MEATLOAF WITH MUSHROOM SAUCE

Ingredients

Meatloaf

- ½ lb lean ground beef
- 1 large egg
- ¼ tsp garlic powder
- ¼ tsp onion powder
- ¼ tsp smoked paprika
- ¼ tsp ground cumin
- ¼ tsp ground mustard seed
- ¼ tsp ground black pepper
- 1 tsp kosher salt
- ¼ tsp worcestershire sauce (optional)
- ¼ cup panko breadcrumbs

Mushroom Sauce

- 1 cup baby bella mushrooms, diced
- ½ cup yellow onion, diced
- 1 tsp garlic, minced
- 1 tsp sherry or balsamic vinegar
- 1 tsp Dijon mustard
- 1 tsp whole mustard
- ½ cup unsalted beef broth
- 1 tbsp unsalted butter (omit if making roux below)
- 1 tbsp parsley, chopped

Roux (optional)

- 1 tbsp unsalted butter
- 2 tsp all-purpose flour

Directions

Combine all the ingredients for the meatloaf and mix thoroughly. Press the mixture into a small mound at the bottom of your Rice Cooker. The mound should be compact and firm. Then, mix together the ingredients for the mushroom sauce (except for the parsley). Add this mixture to the Rice Cooker. Cook until the meatloaf is cooked through, for however many cycles it takes. Remove the lid of the Rice Cooker and let cook for another 10 minutes, uncovered. Remove the meatloaf from the Rice Cooker and set aside.

If making the roux, massage the butter and flour together in a separate bowl. Add the butter and flour to the Rice Cooker and stir with the mushroom sauce. Let cook for another 5 minutes. Add the parsley and stir to combine. Remove from the heat and serve with the meatloaf.

TERIYAKI CHICKEN OVER BROWN RICE

Ingredients

Teriyaki Sauce (if making)

- ½ cup soy sauce
- ¼ cup water
- 2 tbsp mirin
- ¼ cup light brown sugar
- 2 tsp garlic, minced
- 1 tsp ginger, minced

Chicken & Rice

- 2 boneless chicken thighs, chopped
- ¼ cup teriyaki sauce, store-bought or homemade
- ½ cup short grain brown rice
- ½ cup low-sodium chicken or vegetable broth
- ½ cup carrots, cut into strips
- ½ cup green or savoy cabbage, shredded
- 1 tbsp scallion, sliced

Directions

Combine ingredients for teriyaki sauce in a small saucepan on stovetop over low heat. Let simmer 15 minutes, stirring. Combine all ingredients for chicken and rice in Rice Cooker except scallion. Cook 2 cycles, or until chicken is cooked through. Turn off Rice Cooker and add scallion to serve.

INDIAN BIRYANI

Ingredients

Rice

- ½ cup basmati rice
- ½ cup tomato, fresh or canned, diced
- ½ cup yellow onion, minced
- ½ tsp garlic, minced
- 25 pods cardamom
- ½ tsp fenugreek seeds (optional)
- 2 bay leaves
- ¼ tsp ground cinnamon
- ¼ tsp ground mustard seed
- ¼ tsp ground clove
- ¼ tsp ground turmeric
- ¼ tsp ginger, minced
- ½ tsp kosher salt
- 5 oz low-sodium chicken or vegetable broth
- 1 tbsp unsalted butter

Curry Chicken Thighs

- 2 chicken thighs, chopped
- 1 tsp kosher salt
- ½ to 1 tsp curry powder

Topping (optional)

- 2 tbsp plain yogurt

Directions

Combine all ingredients for rice in Rice Cooker and stir to combine. Toss chicken thighs with salt and curry powder and add to Rice Cooker. Cook 2 cycles, or until chicken is fully cooked through. Remove bay leaves before serving. Serve with yogurt, if desired.

PINEAPPLE FRIED RICE

Ingredients

- ¼ cup pineapple, diced
- ½ cup frozen peas and/or carrots
- ¼ cup onion, diced
- 2 tbsp olive oil, divided
- 2 tsp sesame oil, divided
- ½ tsp ginger powder
- ¼ cup green onion, sliced
- ¾ cup short grain brown rice
- 1½ cups chicken broth
- 1 egg, scrambled

Directions

Cook brown rice in the Rice Cooker with the chicken broth. While the rice is cooking, sauté the peas, carrots, and onion on the stovetop with 1 tbsp olive oil and 1 tsp sesame oil until onions are translucent.

Add pineapple, egg, and green onion to stovetop pan. Set ingredients aside. When the rice is finished cooking, heat the remaining tbsp of olive oil and 1 tsp of sesame oil in a pan and add the rice. Stir for about 1 minute before adding other ingredients. Cook for 2-3 minutes and serve immediately.

FARFALLE WITH TURKEY BOLOGNESE

Ingredients

- ½ lb ground turkey
- 1 cup dry farfalle pasta
- ¾ cup tomato, diced, canned, or fresh
- ½ cup yellow onion, diced
- 2 tsp oregano, leaves only, chopped
- 1 tsp thyme, leaves only, chopped
- ½ tsp garlic, minced

- ¼ tsp ground black pepper
- 2 tsp olive oil
- 1 tsp balsamic vinegar
- 1 tsp kosher salt
- ¼ cup unsalted beef or chicken broth
- 1 tbsp basil, chopped
- 1 tbsp parsley, chopped

Directions

Combine all ingredients except parsley and basil in Rice Cooker and stir. Cook, uncovered, 30-40 minutes until turkey is fully cooked through and sauce has cooked down. Break up turkey and stir sauce throughout the cooking cycle to incorporate. Turn off Rice Cooker and add basil and parsley.

SOUTHWESTERN RICE PILAF WITH PINTO BEANS

Ingredients

- ¼ cup long-grain carolina rice
- ½ cup pinto beans
- 2 boneless chicken thighs, chopped
- ½ cup poblano pepper, seeded, diced
- ¼ cup yellow onion, diced
- 1 jalapeno, seeded or unseeded, minced

- 1 tsp garlic, minced
- ¼ tsp ancho chile powder
- ¼ tsp ground cumin
- ¼ tsp ground black pepper
- 1 tsp kosher salt
- 3 oz low-sodium chicken broth

Directions

Combine all ingredients in the Rice Cooker and stir. Cook 2 cycles, or until chicken thighs are fully cooked through.

TUNA AVOCADO POKE BOWL WITH GREEN TEA SUSHI RICE

Ingredients

Sushi Rice

- 1 cup short-grain sushi rice
- 1 tbsp dried wakame seaweed
- 1 tsp matcha green tea powder
- 1 ¼ cups water
- 1 tbsp mirin
- ½ tsp kosher salt
- ½ cup edamame, shelled, frozen

Bowl

- ½ cup carrot, shredded
- 2 tsp scallion, sliced
- ½ avocado, diced
- 1 tsp toasted white sesame seeds

Tuna Poke

- 8 oz yellowfin or albacore tuna, raw, diced
- 1 tbsp soy sauce
- 3 tsp mirin
- 1 tbsp scallion, minced
- 1 tsp garlic, minced
- 1 tsp sesame oil, minced
- 1 tsp sriracha (optional)

Directions

Combine all ingredients for sushi rice in Rice Cooker. Cook 1 cycle. Once rice is finished, combine rice with tuna and all other ingredients for bowl.

THANKSGIVING BOWL

Ingredients

Turkey Meatloaf
- ½ lb ground turkey
- 1 large egg
- 1 tsp kosher salt
- ¼ tsp garlic powder
- ¼ tsp onion powder
- ½ tsp dried rosemary
- ½ tsp dried thyme
- ¼ tsp ground black pepper
- ¼ tsp dried parsley
- ¼ cup panko breadcrumbs

Bowl
- 1 cup sweet potato, small dice
- ¼ cup corn kernels, fresh or frozen
- 1 tbsp sage, sliced
- ½ tsp kosher salt
- ¼ cup dried cranberries
- 1 tsp garlic, minced
- ½ cup low-sodium chicken or vegetable broth
- 1 tbsp fresh parsley, chopped

Directions

Combine all ingredients for turkey meatloaf in a small bowl and mix until well combined. Place into Rice Cooker. Add all ingredients for bowl except parsley in Rice Cooker and stir to combine. Cook 2 cycles. Remove meatloaf from Rice Cooker and slice. Serve with the rest of bowl ingredients and parsley.

CHEESY CHICKEN & MUSHROOM CASSEROLE

Ingredients

- 1 tbsp butter
- 1 clove garlic, minced
- ½ chicken breast, cut into bite sized pieces
- ¼ cup mushrooms, sliced
- ½ cup uncooked jasmine rice

- 1 cup chicken broth
- ¼ cup shredded parmesan cheese
- 2 tbsp italian flat leaf parsley, chopped
- salt and pepper, to taste

Directions

Add butter, garlic, chicken, and mushrooms to the Rice Cooker and turn On. Stir until chicken is browned on all sides. Add rice and chicken broth and then cover with Lid.

Cook until end of cooking cycle. Add shredded parmesan cheese and stir. Let sit with the Lid on for an additional 5 minutes.

Add salt and pepper to taste. Garnish with the chopped parsley and serve immediately.

CAJUN RICE WITH SAUSAGE & SHRIMP

Ingredients

- 1 link smoked sausage, thinly sliced
- 5 shrimp, peeled and deveined
- ¼ cup french onion soup
- ½ cup water
- ¼ cup canned diced tomatoes, drained

- 2 tbsp green pepper, diced
- ¼ cup canned black beans, drained
- ½ cup uncooked long grain rice
- ¼ tsp cajun seasoning

Directions

Add all ingredients except the shrimp to the Rice Cooker and cook for 1 cooking cycle. Add the shrimp.

Let sit 5 minutes and then press cook again. Allow to cook for an additional 10 minutes until the shrimp are cooked through before serving.

MACARONI & CHEESE WITH BROCCOLI

Ingredients

- 1 cup uncooked macaroni pasta
- ¾ cup chicken stock
- ¼ tsp salt
- ¼ cup milk
- ½ cup cheddar cheese, shredded

- ¼ cup part skim mozzarella cheese
- ½ tbsp butter
- ½ cup cooked broccoli florets (optional)
- salt and pepper, to taste

Directions

Put the pasta, chicken stock, milk, and salt in the Rice Cooker and stir. Cover with Lid and turn on the Rice Cooker.

Cook until all the liquid is absorbed. As soon as it's is absorbed, carefully remove the Lid and add the cheese, butter, and stir well.

Close the lid and cook until the cycle is complete and your cooker switches to keep warm. Add broccoli florets.

CHINESE "STIR FRY"

Ingredients

- 1 cup green bell pepper, sliced
- ¾ cup carrot, peeled, sliced
- ½ cup canned bamboo shoots, drained
- ½ yellow onion, sliced
- ½ tsp fresh ginger, minced
- ½ tsp fresh garlic, minced
- 1 cup pork loin, diced

- 3 tbsp soy sauce
- 2 tsp sesame oil
- 2 tsp mirin
- ¼ tsp maple syrup
- ½ cup low-sodium chicken stock
- 2 tsp scallion, sliced

Directions

Combine all ingredients except scallion in Rice Cooker. Cook 1 or 2 cycles, until pork is cooked through. Garnish with scallion. Serve with short grain or jasmine rice, if desired.

Summer Wheat Berry Salad | Page 66-67

RICE & SIDE DISHES

GERMAN POTATO SALAD

Ingredients

Potatoes

- ½ cup yukon potatoes, chopped
- ½ cup low-sodium chicken
  or vegetable stock

Bacon & Dressing

- 4 slices bacon or turkey bacon, chopped
- ¼ cup apple cider vinegar
- ¼ cup drained potato liquid (from above)
- 2 tsp maple syrup
- ½ cup yellow onion, diced
- ¼ tsp ground black pepper
- 1 tbsp parsley, chopped
- 1 wedge lemon (optional)

Directions

Combine potatoes and stock in Rice Cooker. Cook 25-30 minutes, until potatoes are fork-tender. Drain and reserve drained liquid.

Add bacon to medium sauté pan over low heat. Render 5-7 minutes, until well-browned. Drain bacon on paper towels. Add onion and let sauté on low-medium heat until translucent, 3-5 minutes.

Add apple cider vinegar, drained potato liquid, maple syrup, and black pepper. Cook another 5-10 minutes over low-medium heat until mixture has thickened and is bubbling. Add potatoes and cook 1-2 minutes to warm up potatoes.

Remove from heat and toss with chopped bacon, parsley, and juice of 1 lemon wedge, if desired.

HERBED POLENTA

Ingredients

- ½ cup dry polenta
- 1 cup low-sodium chicken or vegetable stock
- ½ tsp kosher salt
- ¼ tsp garlic powder
- ¼ tsp black pepper

- ½ tsp dried rosemary
- ½ tsp dried thyme
- ½ tsp dried parsley

Directions

Combine all ingredients in the Rice Cooker and stir. Cook 1 cycle.

RAISIN & ALMOND SPICED RICE

Ingredients

- 1 cup basmati rice
- ½ cup raisins
- ½ cup sliced almonds
- 2 bay leaves (optional)
- ¼ cup yellow onion, diced
- 1 tbsp unsalted butter
- 2 tsp caraway seeds
- ½ tsp ground cumin

- 2 tsp kosher salt
- 9 oz unsalted low-sodium chicken or vegetable broth
- 1 ¼ cups low-sodium chicken or vegetable stock
- 1 tbsp fried shallots, homemade or store-bought (optional)
- 1 tbsp parsley, chopped

Directions

Combine all ingredients in Rice Cooker and stir. Cook 1 cycle. Remove bay leaves, if needed, prior to serving.

BAKED FARRO "MEATBALLS"

Ingredients

Cooked Farro

- ¾ cup farro
- 1 ½ cup water, low-sodium chicken or unsalted beef stock

Farro Meatballs

- cooked farro (from above)
- ¼ tsp onion powder
- ¼ tsp garlic powder
- 1 dash red chili flakes (optional)
- ½ tsp kosher salt
- ½ tsp dried oregano
- ½ tsp dried thyme
- 1 tbsp parmesan, grated (optional)
- 1 large egg
- ¼ cup panko breadcrumbs

Directions

Combine farro with water or stock in Rice Cooker and cook thoroughly. Remove farro from Rice Cooker and let cool, 5-10 minutes. Preheat oven to 400°F. Combine farro with all other ingredients and mix thoroughly. Place farro mixture in food processor and process until the mixture resembles cornmeal. Form into meatballs. Bake at 400°F for 10-15 minutes until lightly browned on the outside.

 You can substitute these farro meatballs anywhere regular meatballs are used - great for long braises!

TOASTED COCONUT RICE

Ingredients

- ½ cup coconut flakes
- ¾ cup long grain carolina rice
- ½ tsp kosher salt
- 1 tbsp coconut oil
- 1 cup water

Directions

Toast coconut flakes in a small, nonstick sauté pan on low heat until golden brown. Combine coconut with all other ingredients in Rice Cooker and stir. Cook 1 cycle.

THAI COCONUT RICE

Ingredients

- ¾ cup jasmine rice
- ½ cup coconut cream
- 1 cup water
- ¼ tsp sea salt
- ¼ tsp coconut oil

Garnish

- ¼ cup cashews
- ¼ cup golden raisins

Directions

Coat the inside of the Rice Cooker with coconut oil and add the rice, water, and coconut milk to the Rice Cooker.

Cover and turn the Rice Cooker on. Cook for 1 cycle. Garnish with cashews and raisins.

CILANTRO LIME RICE

Ingredients

- 1 tsp olive oil
- ¼ cup chopped onion
- 1 clove garlic, finely chopped
- ¾ cup long grain jasmine rice

- 1 ¼ cup water
- ⅛ tsp sea salt
- 1 tbsp freshly squeezed lime juice
- ⅛ cup cilantro, chopped

Directions

Add olive oil and chopped onion to Rice Cooker then switch On. When onion begins to soften, add the garlic, rice, water and salt. Cook until all the water is absorbed. Fluff rice with a fork.

Stir in lime juice and cilantro and serve immediately.

WILD RICE & MUSHROOM PILAF

Ingredients

- ½ cup wild rice
- 1 cup shiitake mushroom, sliced
- 1 cup baby bella mushrooms, sliced
- ½ tsp kosher salt
- 1 dash ground black pepper
- 1 tsp fresh oregano, chopped
- ½ tsp garlic, minced
- ¾ cup low-sodium chicken stock or water

Directions

Add all ingredients to Rice Cooker and stir. Cook 1 cycle.

FARRO SALAD

Ingredients

Farro

- 1 cup farro
- 1 ¼ cup low-sodium chicken stock or water

Dill Vinaigrette

- ¼ cup dill, chopped
- 2 cloves garlic, chopped
- 2 tsp Dijon mustard
- ¼ cup canola or olive oil
- 2 tbsp lemon juice
- ¼ tsp kosher salt
- 1 dash cane sugar
- 2 dashes ground black pepper

Salad

- 1 cup cooked farro (from above)
- ½ cup radish, sliced thinly on mandoline
- ½ cup celery, chopped
- 2 cups baby kale or spinach
- Dill Vinaigrette, to taste (from left)

Directions

Combine farro and chicken stock in Rice Cooker. Cook 1 cycle. Remove and let cool if desired. Combine all ingredients for dill vinaigrette in blender and blend until smooth. Combine all ingredients for salad in large bowl and toss to combine.

QUINOA TACO BOWL

Ingredients

- ¾ cup quinoa
- ½ cup canned black beans
- 1½ cups chicken or vegetable broth
- ¼ cup pico de gallo or salsa
- ½ sliced avocado
- ¼ cup shredded cheese
- ¼ cup corn
- ½ tbsp taco seasoning (cayenne, cumin, coriander, paprika)
- sour cream, optional
- ½ lime, juiced
- ⅛ tsp sea salt

Directions

Add quinoa and broth to the Rice Cooker. Cook for 20 minutes. Rinse and drain the black beans and add them to the Rice Cooker with the taco seasoning mix, lime, and sea salt.

Serve in a bowl topped with shredded cheese, sliced avocado, corn, and pico de gallo or salsa. Garnish with a drizzle of sour cream, if desired.

VEGETABLE SUSHI

Ingredients

Sushi Rice

- 1 cup short grain sushi rice
- 1 ¼ cups water
- 2 tbsp mirin
- ¼ tsp canola or olive oil

Per Roll

- 1 piece nori wrapping paper
- 2 tbsp sushi rice
- ¼ avocado, sliced lengthwise
- 2 tbsp carrot, sliced into strips
- 2 tbsp mung bean sprouts
- 2 tbsp cucumber, sliced into strips
- ½ tsp scallion, sliced
- ¼ tsp sesame oil
- ¼ tsp toasted sesame seeds
- ½ tsp pickled ginger, chopped (optional)

Directions

Wash rice thoroughly in small bowl until water runs clear. Drain. Combine rice with water, mirin and oil in Rice Cooker. Cook 1 cycle.

For each roll, place nori wrapper shiny side down on bamboo sushi mat. Add sushi rice to form a thin, long rectangle on bottom third of wrapper that extends to both end of the wrapper. Top rice with avocado, carrots, mung bean sprouts, cucumber, scallion, sesame oil, sesame and pickled ginger.

Roll wrapper tightly over filling, using bamboo mat, and squeeze gently to compress roll. Continue to roll and finally seal the end of nori wrapper by dabbing cold water on the end of the nori roll. Slice sushi roll into pieces using a sharp knife that has been run under cold water. Serve with soy sauce, if desired.

SALMON SUSHI

Ingredients

Sushi Rice
- 1 cup short grain sushi rice
- 1 ¼ cups water
- 2 tbsp mirin
- ¼ tsp canola or olive oil

Marinated Salmon
- ½ lb salmon, sliced into thin rectangles roughly the length of nori wrapper
- 1 tbsp mirin
- 1 tbsp rice vinegar
- 1 tbsp soy sauce

- 1 tsp scallion, minced
- ¼ tsp garlic, minced
- ¼ tsp ginger, minced

Per Roll
- 1 square nori wrapper
- 2 tbsp sushi rice
- 1 slice marinated salmon
- ¼ avocado, sliced lengthwise
- 2 tbsp cucumber, sliced into strips
- 1 tsp scallion, sliced
- ¼ tsp toasted sesame seeds

Directions

Wash rice thoroughly in small bowl until water runs clear. Drain. Combine rice with water, mirin and oil in Rice Cooker. Cook 1 cycle. Combine all ingredients for marinated salmon and toss to incorporate. Let marinate 30 minutes.

For each roll, place nori wrapper shiny side down on bamboo sushi mat. Add sushi rice to form a thin, long rectangle on bottom third of wrapper that extends to both end of the wrapper. Top rice with salmon, avocado, cucumber, scallion and sesame seeds.

Roll wrapper tightly over filling, using bamboo mat, and squeeze gently to compress roll. Continue to roll and finally seal the end of nori wrapper by dabbing cold water on the end of the nori roll. Slice sushi roll into pieces using a sharp knife that has been run under cold water. Serve with soy sauce, if desired.

DOLMAS

Ingredients

Rice Filling
- 1 cup long grain rice, dry
- ¼ cup raisins
- ¼ cup pine nuts
- ¼ tsp ground cinnamon
- ¼ tsp dried basil
- ¼ tsp ground cumin
- ¼ tsp garlic powder
- ¼ tsp smoked sweet paprika
- 2 tbsp tomato paste
- ¼ cup fresh mint, chopped
- ¼ cup fresh parsley, chopped
- ¼ cup fresh dill, chopped
- 2 tsp kosher salt

To Cook
- 15-20 grape leaves, drained
- 1-2 cups low-sodium chicken or vegetable broth

Garnish
- 1 lemon, cut into wedges
- 1 tbsp high quality extra virgin olive oil

Directions

Combine ingredients for rice filling in large bowl and mix together thoroughly. Lay grape leaves down on clean surface, shiny side down, and place approximately 2 tsp of rice filling at center. Roll left and right edges of the dolma towards center, tuck the bottom of the grape leaf under the rice filling, and roll into compact cylindrical shape (like a burrito).

Layer 2 layers of dolmas in Rice Cooker. Pour in enough chicken broth to cover dolmas and cook 1 cycle. Gently open one dolma to test rice doneness. If needed, add more chicken broth and cook another cycle. Let cool. Serve dolmas either warm or cold with lemon wedges and drizzle of olive oil.

PESTO PEARLED COUSCOUS

Ingredients

Parsley Pesto
- 2 cups parsley, leaves only
- 1 tsp garlic, sliced
- ¼ cup pine nuts
- ¼ cup parmesan cheese, grated
- ½ cup extra virgin olive oil
- ½ tsp kosher salt

Pearled Couscous
- 1 package (6oz) pearled couscous
- 1 ½ cups low-sodium chicken stock or water

Directions

Combine all ingredients for pesto in a blender and blend until smooth. Combine couscous and chicken stock in Rice Cooker and cook 1 cycle. Remove couscous from Rice Cooker and toss with pesto, to taste.

COUSCOUS SALAD

Ingredients

- 1 cup of couscous
- 1 ½ cups vegetable or chicken stock
- ¼ cup crumbled goat cheese
- ¼ small red onion, diced
- 10 cherry or grape tomatoes, halved

- ¼ cup sliced almonds
- ¼ cup golden raisins
- ⅛ cup olive oil
- salt and pepper, to taste

Directions

Place the couscous and stock in the Rice Cooker. Cover with Lid and switch On. Once the cycle is complete, transfer cooked couscous to a large bowl.

Toss with remaining ingredients and serve.

SUMMER WHEAT BERRY SALAD

Ingredients

Wheat Berries
- 1 cup dry wheat berry
- 1 ½ cups low-sodium chicken stock or water

Basil Vinaigrette
- 2 cups basil, chopped
- ¼ tsp garlic, minced
- 2 tbsp lime juice
- ⅓ cup extra virgin olive oil
- ½ tsp Dijon mustard
- ½ tsp kosher salt
- 1 dash cane sugar
- 1 dash ground black pepper

Salad
- 1 cup cooked wheat berries (from above)
- ½ cup corn kernels, fresh or frozen
- 1 cup fennel, shaved thinly on mandoline
- ¼ cup celery, diced
- 10 grape tomatoes, halved
- 1 cup spinach
- Basil Vinaigrette, to taste (from above)

Directions

Combine wheat berries with stock in Rice Cooker. Cook 1 cycle. Combine all ingredients for basil vinaigrette in a blender and blend until smooth. Combine all ingredients for salad in large bowl and toss to combine.

RICE COOKER KIMCHI

Ingredients

- 3 cups napa or savoy cabbage, chopped
- ½ cup daikon, peeled, halved, sliced thinly
- 2 Thai bird's eye chiles, sliced thinly (optional)
- 1 tsp fresh garlic, minced
- 1 tsp fresh ginger, minced
- 2 tsp scallion, sliced

- 2 tsp Korean red pepper flakes
- 2 tsp kosher salt
- ¾ tsp cane sugar
- 2 tbsp rice vinegar
- ½ cup cold water

Directions

Combine all ingredients in Rice Cooker and place on "Keep Warm" setting for 12 hours. Remove from Rice Cooker and place into sanitized canning jar. Seal. Let stand at room temperature for 3-5 days, depending on taste preference. Make sure to shake jar a few times a day to ensure proper coating of ingredients with pickling liquid.

White Bean & Escarole Soup | Page 74-75

SOUPS

TOFU SHIITAKE MISO SOUP

Ingredients

- 2 cups water
- 1 tbsp sweet white miso
- ½ cup shiitake mushrooms, sliced
- 1 cup tofu, cut into cubes
- 1 tsp kosher salt
- 1 tbsp scallion, sliced

Directions

Combine water and white miso in small bowl. Whisk thoroughly before adding to Rice Cooker. Add shiitake, tofu, and salt to Rice Cooker and stir. Cook 15-20 minutes until shiitake is cooked through. Add scallion and stir.

Miso naturally settles at the bottom of the bowl, so stir before serving.

SPICED LENTIL SOUP

Ingredients

- ½ cup yellow onion, diced
- ¼ cup carrot, diced
- ¼ cup celery, diced
- 1 tsp garlic, minced
- ¼ cup dry green lentils
- ½ cup diced tomato, canned
  - fire roasted variety preferable
- ¼ tsp smoked sweet paprika

- ¼ tsp dried thyme
- ¼ tsp ground curry powder
- 1 tsp kosher salt
- 2 bay leaves (optional)
- 1 dash cayenne pepper (optional)
- 1 ½ cups low-sodium chicken
  or vegetable broth
- 1 tbsp fresh dill, chopped

Directions

Combine all ingredients except dill in Rice Cooker and stir. Cook, uncovered, 25-30 minutes until lentils are fully cooked through. Add dill and stir.

WHITE BEAN & ESCAROLE SOUP

Ingredients

- ½ cup yellow onion, diced
- ¼ cup carrot, diced
- ¼ cup celery, diced
- 1 cup white beans, drained, rinsed
- 1 tsp fresh rosemary, stemmed, minced
- 2 tsp garlic, minced

- 2 tbsp parmesan, grated
- 1 tsp fresh thyme, leaves only
- 1 tsp kosher salt
- ¼ tsp ground black pepper
- 1 ½ cups low-sodium chicken stock
- 1 cup escarole, sliced

Directions

Combine all ingredients except escarole in Rice Cooker and cook 25-35 minutes. Remove lid and add escarole. Cook another 3-5 minutes until escarole is wilted. Serve with extra parmesan and ground black pepper, if desired.

CHICKEN NOODLE SOUP

Ingredients

- 1 tsp olive oil
- ¼ onion, finely chopped
- ¼ carrot, sliced
- 1 tsp garlic, minced
- ½ boneless chicken breast, diced in ½" cubes

- 1 ½ cups chicken broth
- 2 tsp parsley, finely chopped
- ¼ cup spiral pasta
- salt and pepper, to taste

Directions

Pour the olive oil into the Rice Cooker and add onion, carrot, garlic, and cook with the Lid on for a few minutes until onions soften.

Remove Lid and add the pasta, chicken, broth, parsley, salt, and pepper. Stir to combine and then cover with the Lid. After 5 minutes, remove the Lid and stir.

You may need to switch the cooker On for an additional cooking cycle. Re-cover and cook until the pasta is tender.

TURKEY CHILI

Ingredients

- 8 oz ground turkey
- 2 tbsp olive oil
- 7.5 oz of canned black beans
- 7.5 oz of canned kidney beans
- 1 tbsp chili powder
- 1 tbsp tomato paste
- ½ cup canned diced tomatoes

- 3 tbsp chili seasoning
- salt and pepper, to taste sour cream, (optional)
- ½ lime, juiced
- ⅛ tsp sea salt
- cheddar cheese, shredded
- scallions, sliced

Directions

Place raw ground turkey in Rice Cooker with the olive oil, turn On and let it run until fully cooked, stirring occasionally. Once fully cooked through, drain excess fat.

Add beans, diced tomatoes, tomato paste, and stir. Add in all seasonings and let simmer for another full cycle in the Rice Cooker.

Top your chili with the cheddar cheese and sliced scallions.

THAI RED CURRY CHICKEN

Ingredients

- 2 tbsp Thai red curry paste
- 1½ cups coconut milk
- 1 tsp ginger, minced
- 1 clove garlic, minced
- ½ cup snow peas, rinsed

- ½ yellow onion, sliced
- ½ cup bamboo shoots
- ¼ cup red bell pepper, chopped
- soy sauce, to taste
- ½ chicken breast, cut into ½" pieces

Directions

In a bowl, mix the curry paste and coconut milk. Place the mixture into the Rice Cooker with all ingredients except chicken and soy sauce and stir to combine.

Season to taste with soy sauce and then add chicken. Cover the Rice Cooker and switch On. After 20 minutes, carefully remove the Lid and stir.

Re-cover and cook for 10 more minutes.

Chardonnay & Cardamom Poached Pears | Page 88-89

DESSERTS

WHOLE WHEAT BREAD PUDDING

Ingredients

- 2 cups whole wheat baguette, chopped into pieces
- ¾ cup heavy cream
- ⅔ cup cane sugar
- 2 large eggs
- 1 tsp kosher salt
- ¼ tsp ground cinnamon
- ¼ tsp ground cloves
- ¼ tsp ground allspice
- ¼ tsp ground nutmeg
- 1 tbsp high quality rum (optional)
- ¼ cup raisins

Directions

Add baguette to Rice Cooker. In small bowl, whisk together cream, sugar, eggs, salt, cinnamon, cloves, allspice, nutmeg, and rum. Pour over baguette pieces. Top with raisin. Cook in Rice Cooker, 2-3 cycles until bread has absorbed all the moisture of the cream. Serve warm or chilled.

APPLE CRUMBLE

Ingredients

Stewed Apples

- 3 cups peeled, chopped apples
- 2 tbsp unsalted butter
- ¼ cup light brown sugar

Oat Crumble

- ½ cup quick-cooking old fashioned rolled oats
- ¼ cup all-purpose flour
- 3 tbsp unsalted butter
- ½ cup light brown sugar
- ½ tsp kosher salt
- ¼ cup water

Directions

Combine all ingredients for stewed apples in Rice Cooker. Cook 1 cycle. Remove and keep warm. Combine all ingredients for oat crumble in Rice Cooker and stir. Cook 2 cycles. Remove Rice Cooker lid and stir. Leave mixture on "Keep Warm" setting until the bottoms of the oat crumble crisps and turns golden brown. Add apples and stir together. Serve with ice cream, if desired.

MANGO STICKY RICE

Ingredients

Sticky Rice

- 1 cup glutinous rice (sticky rice)
- 1 cup water
- ½ cup full fat coconut milk
- 2 tbsp cane sugar

Mango Sticky Rice

- 3 cups fresh mango, peeled, seeded, chopped
- cooked sticky rice, from above
- ½ cup coconut flakes (optional)
- 2 tbsp sweetened condensed milk (optional)

Directions

Combine ingredients for sticky rice in Rice Cooker and stir. Cook 1 cycle. If using coconut flakes, toast lightly over low heat in small sauté pan until golden brown. Add coconut flakes to sticky rice and stir. Remove sticky rice from Rice Cooker and add fresh mango on top. Drizzle with sweetened condensed milk, if desired.

CHARDONNAY & CARDAMOM POACHED PEARS

Ingredients

- 2 Bosc pears, peeled
- ½ cup high-quality chardonnay
- ½ cup water
- 2 tbsp cane sugar

- 1 tbsp whole green cardamom
- 1 tsp whole cloves
- 1 cinnamon stick

Directions

Combine all ingredients in Rice Cooker. Cook, uncovered, stirring to keep pears submerged in water through cooking process for approximately 15 to 20 minutes. Serve whole with a few spoonfuls of syrup.

CHOCOLATE CAKE

Ingredients

- ½ cup cane sugar
- 6 tbsp unsalted butter
- 1 egg
- 1 tsp vanilla extract

- ½ tsp baking powder
- 1 cup all-purpose flour
- ¼ cup cocoa powder
- ½ cup milk or non-dairy milk

Directions

Place sugar in large bowl. Melt butter over low heat in sauté pan and pour into sugar. Whisk thoroughly, 1-2 minutes, until fully combined. Add egg and vanilla extract and whisk again.

Combine baking powder, flour and cocoa powder in a small bowl and whisk to combine. Mix into sugar mixture in 3 steps, alternating with milk. Whisk mixture until smooth and to break up any clumps. Place approximately 1 cup of mixture into Rice Cooker and cook 1 cycle.

Test doneness at the center of the cake - if needed, cook another cycle. Serve with whipped cream and strawberries, if desired.

CHEESECAKE WITH GRAHAM CRACKER CRUMBLE

Ingredients

Cheesecake

- 8 oz (1 package) cream cheese, warmed to room temperature
- 2 large eggs
- ⅓ cup cane sugar
- ½ lemon, juiced
- ¾ cup heavy cream
- ¼ cup all-purpose flour
- 2 tsp cornstarch

Graham Cracker Crumble

- ¼ cup graham crackers, crumbled
- 2 tbsp light brown sugar
- 2 tbsp butter, melted
- 1 tbsp pecan or walnut pieces, chopped (optional)
- 1 dash ground cinnamon
- 1 dash ground clove
- ½ cup coconut flakes (optional)
- 2 tbsp sweetened condensed milk (optional)

Directions

Combine cream cheese, eggs, sugar, and lemon juice in a small bowl or stand mixer. Mix with whisk by hand or with whisk on stand mixer. Add heavy cream and continue to mix until smooth. Slowly add all-purpose flour and cornstarch and mix until smooth. Pour 1 cup of batter into Rice Cooker and cook 2 cycles. Remove from Rice Cooker and refrigerate until cool and firm. Makes 2 cheesecakes.

Preheat oven to 350°F. Combine all ingredients for graham cracker crumble in small bowl and mix thoroughly to combine. Spread on quarter sheet tray lined with parchment and bake approximately 10 minutes, until crunchy. Remove from oven and let cool. Serve with cheesecake slices.

RICE PUDDING

Ingredients

- ½ cup rice
- 1 ¾ cups milk, divided
- ⅓ cup coconut or cane sugar

- 1 tsp cinnamon
- ¼ tsp nutmeg
- ½ tsp pure vanilla extract

Directions

Add the rice, 1 cup milk, sugar, and vanilla to the Rice Cooker. Cook for 1 cycle.

When the Rice Cooker finishes cooking, stir in the cinnamon, nutmeg, and raisins along with the remaining ¾ cup of milk.

PINEAPPLE UPSIDE DOWN CAKE

Ingredients

- 1 ½ slices fresh pineapple, ½" thick
- 1 tbsp dark brown sugar
- 1 tbsp unsalted butter
- ½ cup buttermilk pancake mix
- 2 tbsp dark brown sugar
- ½ cup milk or non-dairy milk
- 2 tbsp pineapple juice

Directions

Sprinkle 1 tbsp dark brown sugar at bottom of Rice Cooker. Add butter to Rice Cooker. Place pineapple in one layer on top of butter and sugar. Combine buttermilk pancake mix with 2 tbsp dark brown sugar, milk and pineapple juice. Whisk to combine and pour over pineapple slices. Cook 1 cycle. Remove lid and cook 1 more cycle. Remove from Rice Cooker and let cool 5 minutes. Carefully invert onto clean plate.

Spray Rice Cooker with nonstick spray to ensure easy inverting.

BANANA BREAD

Ingredients

- 2 medium bananas, very ripe, peeled
- 1 large egg
- ⅔ cup cane sugar
- ¼ cup ricotta cheese
- 1 tbsp coconut oil
- ¼ cup walnuts or pecans, chopped (optional)

- 1 tsp vanilla extract
- ½ tsp kosher salt
- 1 tsp baking powder
- 2 tsp rum (optional)
- 1½ cups all-purpose flour
- 2 tbsp maple syrup
- 1 medium banana, sliced

Directions

Place bananas in medium bowl and mash thoroughly with spatula. Add egg and continue to mash. Add sugar, ricotta, and oil and stir to combine. Add oil, walnuts, vanilla extract, salt, baking powder, rum, and flour to bowl and mix thoroughly. Pour approximately 1 cup of mixture into Rice Cooker. Cook 1 cycle. Carefully invert onto clean plate. Transfer cake back into Rice Cooker, with the previous top side now facing down. Cook 1 cycle. Remove from Rice Cooker and garnish with sliced bananas and maple syrup, if desired.

INDEX

Rice Cooker Kimchi | Page 68-69